TREE FLORA OF MINDANAO STATE UNIVERSITY MAGUINDANAO CAMPUS

GINDOL REY A. LIMBARO

and

MARK ERICKSON A. LAURIE

COLLEGE OF FORESTRY AND ENVIRONMENTAL STUDIES
Mindanao State University – Maguindanao
Dalican, Datu Odin Sinsuat, Maguindanao
09953693867 / 09383613757
limbarogindol@gmail.com

ABSTRACT

The term "Flora "pertains to all plant life present in a particular region or time and tree is one of the types of flora. This study was conducted to find out the existing tree species found thriving at the MSU – Maguindanao Campus, Datu Odin Sinsuat, Maguindanao Province, moreover to determine the average height, average diameter, conservation status, ecological status, importance value and Shannon-Weiner Diversity Index. The method used was transect walk with 3 stations with a total sample area of forty two (42) hectare. Results showed that there are three thousand five hundred eighty eight (3,588) individual of trees in the study site of forty two (42) hectare tree species with (25) families and (75) tree species. Conservation status with (30) vulnerable, (14) least concern, (12) critically endangered, (9) endangered, (3) data deficient, (3) other wildlife species, (2) not evaluated, (1) threatened, (1) near threatened. Ecological status; (47) endemic, (26) exotic, and (2) invasive. The dominant species with high importance value were (*Swietenia mahogany*) **Mahogany (14.39)**, (*Mangiferaindica*) **Mango (12.85)**, (*Gmelinaarborea*) **Yemane (6.23)**.The Shannon-Weiner diversity index was 2.59 that is equivalent to a moderate diversity. These trees surround the area of Mindanao State University – Maguindanao and it should be conserved and protected for the sustainability of vegetation or habitats for other life forms therein.

Keywords: Tree Flora, Conservation Status, Ecological Status, Importance Value

INTRODUCTION

Philippines belong to the tropical rain forest country and one of the richest countries in terms of natural resources. Both flora and fauna have high numbers of population and species before but gradually vanishing as human kind rapidly dominates in inhabiting and utilizing trees in the forest.

The biodiversity of the Philippines is commensally and highly unique. Its moist tropical habitat supports many thousands of animals and plants species of which a large number is endemic (Henry, 2000).The Philippines has been described by an international group of conservation as the hottest of the 25 so called biodiversity hot spots in the world. Perhaps, rightly so far after all, the pearl of the orient seas has already last 97 % of its original vegetation and has more critically-endangered wildlife than any other country. Hotspots are with the least number of species found in an exclusive ecosystem, and an alarming high degree of threat these species face. (Heading Nature's Cry: R.A 9147). Moreover, trees are the lungs of the earth; they absorb carbon dioxide that is being exhausted by the automobiles, plant corporations and factories daily. In connection with it is the threat that the trees have faced currently as accompanied with different destructive factors that harm the endemic and native species in the country just like human abusive activities like kaingin, logging, mining and quarrying, rapid increased of population that leads to increase of demands in forest products and continuous irresponsible extraction and exploitation of natural resources in the forest.

Land conversion and irresponsible utilization of natural resources are the specific causes of the said threats, these activities will continually destroy the habitat of wildlife species and the forest trees itself, this might result to the extinction of both flora and fauna species if unabated. In connection, A Forty two (42) hectare total land study area in Mindanao State University – Maguindanao Campus is blessed with biodiversity both flora (plants) and fauna (animals). Tree Flora significantly contributes to the environment especially in mitigating climate change. It also provides protection and habitat to other flora and fauna. But due to lack of studies regarding the statuses of the tree flora species in MSU – Maguindanao, it is highly recommended to have Assessments and Inventory of trees in the said area in order to determine, *what are the current statuses of the tree species present in the area?* Therefore this research in determining the official checklist of tree flora in MSU Maguindanao that would surely serve as a baseline study for further research is very significant in order to monitor the existence or diversity of the trees both native and introduced tree flora species in a local basis and to come up with an immediate strategic plan for the salvation and conservation of the remaining tree flora species. The study was conducted from the month of October up to the month of November 2019.

OBJECTIVE OF THE STUDY

The general objective of the study was to find out the existing tree flora found thriving at the MSU – Maguindanao Campus, Datu Odin Sinsuat, Maguindanao and determining their statuses. Specifically, the study aims:

1. To determine the species and families of trees existing at MSU –

Maguindanao Campus.

2. To determine the average diameter and average height per tree species in MSU –   Maguindanao Campus.

3. To determine the Conservation and Ecological Status of the tree species existing in the study area (Based in IUCN-International Union for Conservation of Nature)

4. To determine the frequency and the Importance value of the trees existing in the area.

5. To determine the Shannon –Weiner Diversity Index of the trees existing in the study area.

METHODOLOGY

MATERIALS

The following materials, paraphernalia, and devices used in conduct of the study are Ball pen, Record book, DSLR camera, Smart Phone, Diameter tape, Biltmore stick, land area measurement mobile app, geo-camera mobile app, google earth, google map, reference book for checklists and authentication, laptop, and smart measure mobile application.

TIME AND PLACE OF THE STUDY AREA

The research study was conducted at Mindanao State University - Maguindanao Campus, Dalican, Datu Odin Sinsuat Municipality, Maguindanao Province. It was a two weeks assessment startedfrom October 20, 2019 to November 5, 2019 to gather significant and relevant data referring to various trees species existing in the area.

Physiological Description of the Study Area

MSU-Maguindanao Campus is located in the Municipality of Datu Odin Sinsuat, Maguindanao Province. The said area now was delighted with different diversity of flora and fauna.The area was planted before with trees like Rain tree, Mahogany, teak, kapok and Mango which currently provide vegetation, shades and habitat for birds and other species of plants and animals.

Physiography

a. **Topography of the Area**

The study area was located at MSU-Maguindanao, Dalican Datu Odin Sinsuat with the elevation Range more or less than 22 meters (72.2 feet).. The MSU MAGUINDANAO Student Village was the base camp of the conduct of the study and it would just takea few minutes to reach the boundaries of the study area only by hiking and trekking.

b. Vegetative cover of the Study Area

Vegetative cover of the study site characterized by the existences of multifarious vegetation, such as; trees, shrub, herbs, grasses, ferns, and vines. This is a great indicator ofa continuous and persistent existence of flora species.

c. Current Land Use

Currently, land conversion into educational buildings, forestation and agriculture were the three activities of the faculty, staffs, students and the administration that being observed in the area. Agricultural crops, timber poaching, fish ponds, fruit trees production, vermi-compost, fresh milk from livestock and seedling production were their specific activities. These were their alternative way in coping up as another source of incomefor MSU-Maguindanao in sustaining the needs of the said Campus.

Accessibility of the Study area

MSU-Maguindanao is a thirty minutes ride from Cotabato City to Tacurong City or General Santos City. To reach the study area, you need to walk, hike or ride a vehicle from the main gate near the national highway.

Assessment Procedure

Early morning at MSU – MAGUINDANAO reconnaissance was done first. After that the first activity was the final procedure for assessment conducted. All trees species inside the Campus with the diameter of at least 5 centimetres up were recorded and documented. Identification was done through the assistance of expert or experienced dendrologist (Retired Prof. LeopoldoRemollo),as well as the use of reference books and published scientific articles through the internet. The identified tree species were classified into Common name, Scientific and Family name, conservation and ecological status, importance value and diversity index using the formula of Shannon-Weiner Diversity Index.

Collection of Data

All trees with 5 cm and above were recorded and documented; photographs were done on its habitat, leaves, stem and bark, flowers and fruits. The diameter and height per tree species were also recorded. The identification of species was done with the help of the expert in taxonomy and dendrology.

Analysis of Data

Raw data were encoded in excel form, to solve its Frequency, relative frequency, relative density, importance value and software in Shannon Weiner Diversity index to analyzed the result of the study. The following are the formula used in the study.

Relative density (RDi)= $\dfrac{\text{no. of species(ni)}}{\text{Total no. of all species}}$ X 100

Frequency (fi)= $\dfrac{\text{no. of stations a species occurs}}{\text{Total no. of area}}$

Relative frequency (RFi) = $\dfrac{\text{frequency of a species (Fi)}}{\text{Total frequency of all species}}$ x 100

Importance Value = $\dfrac{\text{Relative Frequency + Relative Density}}{2}$

Shannon –Weiner Diversity Index Formula (Software)

Shannon index= (no.of species/total no. Of populationw/dollar sign)*LN(no.of species/total no.populationw/dollar sign)

RESULTS AND DISCUSSION

The data were presented in tabular form followed by textual discussion.

Table 1 showed that there were seventy five (75) tree species under twenty five (25) families. Fabaceae has 11 species, Moraceae has 10 species, Euphorbiaceae has 7 species and Anacardiaceae has 6 species. Conservation status with thirty (30) vulnerable, fourteen (14) least concern, twelve (12) critically endangered, nine (9) endangered, (3) three data deficient, three (3) other wildlife species, two (2) not evaluated, (1) one threatened and one (1) near threatened. Ecological status of: forty seven (47) endemic, twenty six (26) exotic and two (2) invasive.

FAMILY		COMMON NAME		SCIENTIFIC NAME	CONSERVATION/ECOLOGICAL STATUS
1.	Anacardiaceae	1.	Mangga Manila	*Mangifera indica*	Vulnerable / Endemic
		2.	ManggaPiko	*Mangifera sylvatica F.-Vill.*	Vulnerable / Endemic
		3.	ManggaNative	*Mangifera indica*	Vulnerable / Endemic
		4.	ManggaHuani	*Mangifera odorataGriff*	Endangered / Endemic
		5.	Dao	*Dracontamelon dao*	Critically Endangered / Endemic
		6.	Siniguelas	*Spondias purpurea*	Vulnerable / Exotic
2.	Araucariaceae	7.	Norfolk island pine	*Araucaria heterophylla*	Vulnerable / Exotic
3.	Annonaceae	8.	Guayabano	*Annona muricata*	Vulnerable/ Exotic
		9.	Indian tree	*Polyalthia longifolia*	Vulnerable/ Exotic
		10.	Ilang-ilang	*Cananga odorata*	Threatened /Exotic
4.	Araliaceae	11.	Malapapaya	*Polyscias nodosa*	Endangered / Endemic
5.	Bignoniaceae	12.	African tulip	*Spathodea campanulata*	Least concern and Invasive
6.	Caesalpiniaceae	13.	Golden Shower	*Cassia fistula*	Vulnerable/ Exotic
		14.	Sibukaw	*Caesalpinia sappan*	Least Concern/ Endemic
7.	Clusiaceae	15.	Mangosteen	*Garcinia mangostana*	Not Evaluated / Endemic
8.	Combretaceae	16.	Lanipau	*Terminalia foetidissima*	Near Threatened / Exotic
		17.	Calamansa-nai	*Terminalia calamansanai*	Critically Endangered / Endemic
9.	Dipterocarpa-ceae	18.	Yakalsaplungan	*Hopea plagata*	Endangered / Endemic
		19.	White lauan	*Shorea contorta*	Critically Endangered / Endemic
10.	Ebenaceae	20.	Kamagong	*Diospyros blancoi*	Critically Endangered/ Endemic
11.	Euphorbiaceae	21.	Alim	*Melanolepsis multiglandulosa*	Least concern and Endemic
		22.	Para rubber	*Hevea brasiliensis*	Least Concern / Exotic
		23.	Binunga	*Macaranga tanarius*	Endangered/Endemic
		24.	Banato	*Mallotus philippinensis*	Data Deficient/ Endemic
		25.	Lumbang	*Aleurites moluccanus*	Least Concern / Exotic
		26.	Malabagang	*Glochidion album*	Vulnerable / Endemic
		27.	Palosanto	*Bursera graveolens*	Endangered / Endemic
12.	Fabaceae	28.	Rain tree	*Samanea saman*	Not Evaluated / Endemic

		#	Common Name	Scientific Name	Status/Origin
		29.	Ipil – ipil	*Leucaena leucocephala*	Least Concern/Exotic
		30.	AnchoanDilau	*Pseudocassia spectabilis*	Least Concern/ Invassive
		31.	Fire tree	*Delonix regia*	Vulnirable/ Endemic
		32.	Sampalok	*Tamarindus indica*	Least Concern / Exotic
		33.	Ipil	*Instia bijuga*	Endangered /Endemic
		34.	Kupang	*Parkia timoriana*	Critically Endangered/ Exotic
		35.	Kamachile	*Pithecello biumdulce*	Critically Endangered/ Exotic
		36.	Narra	*Pterocarpus indicus*	Critically Endangered/ Exotic
		37.	Mangium	*Acacia mangium*	Vulnerable / Exotic
		38.	Saraca	*Saracaindica*	Vulnerable / Exotic
13.	Fagaceae	39.	Phil. Chestnut	*Castanopsis philippinensis*	Other Wildlife Species / Endemic
14.	Lamiaceae	40.	Yemane	*Gmelina arborea*	Least Concern / Exotic
		41.	Molave	*Vitex parviflora*	Critically Endangered /Endemic
		42.	Teak	*Tectona grandis*	Critically Endangered / Exotic
15.	Lecythiclac eae	43.	Botong	*Barringtoniaasiatica*	Least Concern/ Endemic
16.	Lauraceae	44.	Avocado	*Persia americana*	Vulnerable/ Exotic
		45.	Sablut	*Litseaperotete*	Vulnerable / Endemic
17.	Malvaceae	46.	Anilau-lalaki	*Columbia longipetiolataMerr.*	Vulnerable/ Endemic
		47.	Durian Tree	*Duriozibethinus*	Vulnerable/ Endemic in SEA
		48.	Cacao	*Theobroma cacao*	Vulnerable/ Exotic
		49.	Kapok	*Ceibapentandra*	Vulnerable/ Endemic in SEA
		50.	Tan – ag	*Kleinhoviahospita*	Vulnerable / Endemic
18.	Meliaceae	51.	Neem tree	*Azadirachtaindica*	Vulnerable / Exotic
		52.	Igyo	*Dysoxylumgaudich adianum*	Vulnerable/ Endemic
		53.	Lansones	*Lansiumdomesticum*	Vulnerable / Endemic
		54.	Santol	*Sandoricumkoetjape*	Vulnerable / Endemic
		55.	Mahogany	*Sweiteniamahogani*	Endangered / Exotic

19.	Moraceae	56.	Alangas	*Ficusheteropoda*	Least concern /Endemic
		57.	Antipolo	*Artocarpusblancoi*	Data Deficient/ Endemic
		58.	Hagimit	*Ficusminahassae*	Critically Endangered/ Endemic
		59.	Jackfruit	*Artocarpusheterophyllus*	Least Concern/ Endemic in SEA
		60.	Niog–niogan	*Ficuspsedopalma*	Endangered / Endemic
		61.	Kalokoi	*Ficuscaliosa*	Critically Endangered/ Endemic
		62.	Tangisangbayawak	*Ficusvariegata*	Other Threatened Species/ Endemic
		63.	Kamansi	*Artocarpuscamansi*	Vulnerable/ Endemic
		64.	Hauili	*Ficusseptica*	Critically Endangered/ Endemic
		65.	Indian Rubber Tree	*Ficuselasticadecora*	Vulnerable/ Exotic
20.	Myrtaceae	66.	Bayabas	*Psidiumguajava*	Vulnerable/ Endemic in SEA
		67.	Bagras	*Eucalyptus deglupta*	Endangered/ Endemic
		68.	Red River Gum	*Eucalyptus camaldulensis*	Data Deficient / Exotic
		69.	Tambis	*Syzygiumaqueum*	Vulnerable / Endemic
21.	Rutaceae	70.	Pomelo	*Citrus maxima*	Vulnerable / Enddemic
		71.	MatangAraw	*Melicopetriphylla (Lam.) Merr*	Other Threatened Species/ Endemic
22.	Rubiaceae	72.	Bangkal	*Naucleaorientalis*	Vulnerable/Endemic
23.	Sapindaceae	73.	Rambutan	*Nepheliumlappaceum*	Least Concern / Exotic
24.	Sapotaceae	74.	Caimito	*Chrysophyllumcainito*	Vulnerable/ Exotic
25.	Ulmaceae	75.	Hanagdong	*Tremagrevel Baill.*	Least Concern/ Endemic
25 Families		75 species			

Table 1. LIST OF TREES AND THE CONSERVATION AND ECOLOGICAL STATUS

Table 2.The Average Height and Average Diameter of trees in three study sites of MSU-Maguindanao

	SPECIES	Ave. Height. (m)	Ave. Diameter. (cm)
1.	Acacia mangium	28.9	8.433333333
2.	African Tulip	25.75847339	38.43816527
3.	Alim	25.5125	6.779166667
4.	Alangas	12.73666667	16.8725
5.	Antipolo	25.57222222	32.63333333
6.	Anulailalaki	9.4	2.45
7.	Ansuandilaw	15.99714286	6.566666667
8.	Avocado	16.74166667	11.81666667
9.	Bayabas	15.95	17.58214286
10.	Bagras	26	10.25714286
11.	Banato	10.83333333	2.522222222
12.	Bangkal	23.095	20.75222222
13.	Botong	22.4	7.366666667
14.	Binunga	14.33333333	5.522222222
15.	Caimito	21.47083333	22.51111111
16.	Cacao	14.3	2.833333333
17.	Dao	27.475	32.75
18.	Durian	18.6	5.816666667
19.	Fire tree	23.0125	30.81388889
20.	Golden Shower	16.69	4.476666667
21.	Guayabano	9.015629877	9.680349313
22.	Yemane	28.18070714	46.72860065
23.	Hanagdong	25.90052632	20.93964912
24.	Hagimit	6	7.666666667
25.	Hauili	19.425	14.15

No.	Species		
26.	Ipil-ipil	14.33108466	16.24920635
27.	Ipil	17.75555556	5.859259259
28.	Igyo	27.56666667	9.488888889
29.	Indian tree	23.02402402	15.73289957
30.	Indian rubber tree	13.6	5.444444444
31.	Ilang – ilang	38.9	7.3
32.	Jackfruit	17.19487923	20.60972222
33.	Kamagong	20.28461538	8.771794872
34.	Kamatchili	19.17	5.72
35.	Kamansi	21.47733333	25.85555556
36.	Calamansanai	34.15	26.53333333
37.	Kalukoi	19.1	6.411111111
38.	Kapok	25.42916667	30.13611111
39.	Kupang	28.35	6.383333333
40.	Lansones	19.45	3.65
41.	Lukban/pomelo	14.88492424	17.01712121
42.	Lumbang	30	21.33333333
43.	Mahogany	24.64453704	**51.07961888**
44.	Mangosteen	17.5	6.483333333
45.	Malabagang	8.2	3.6
46.	Mangga Group	17.00365468	36.27755773
47.	Malapapaya	15.265625	7.554166667
48.	Matangaraw	12.3	3.233333333
49.	Molave	24.65	4.916666667
50.	Narra	33.24180556	36.62572797
51.	Neem tree	16.084375	18.43333333
52.	Niog – niogan	7.1	2
53.	Norfolk pine	14.89166667	9.894444444
54.	Para rubber	20.17844444	19.22666667

55. Palosanto	20.4	11.86666667
56. Philippine Chesnut	10.1	5
57. Rain tree	46.30360683	**74.27189263**
58. Rambutan	13.8125	10.20833333
59. Red river gum	23.30434783	14.11594203
60. Santol	19.65972222	29.33611111
61. Sablut	18.6	3.266666667
62. Sampalok	21.47857143	35.55079365
63. Saraca	18.6	3.266666667
64. Sibukaw	11	3
65. Sinigwilas	15.2	4.812121212
66. Tambis	14.8	4.866666667
67. Tangisangbayawak	24.83972222	35.05083333
68. Lanipau	31.73125	**102.7666667**
69. Tan – ag	21.81695804	13.67983683
70. Teak	17.27083333	36.56666667
71. White lauan	21.8	10.50666667
72. YakalSaplongan	14.6	3.266666667

Table   2   showed   that   Lanipau (*Terminaliafoetidissima*) has the highest average diameter of 102.76 cm, Rain tree (*Samaneasaman*) has 74.2 cm and Mahogany 51.07 cm. Rain tree (*Samaneasaman*) has the highest average height of   46.3   meters, Ilang-ilang (*Canangaodorata)*   has   38.9   m   and   Narra (*Pterocarpusindicus)*has 33.24 meters.

Table 3.Numberof individuals per species and Importance Value of trees in MSU- Maguindanao Campus.

SPECIES	No. individual	Frequency(fi)	Relative Density (Rdi)	Relative Frequency (Rfi)	Importance Value	Rank
1. Mangium	1	0.333333333	0.02787068	0.787401575	0.407636127	60
2. African Tulip	48	1	1.337792642	2.362204724	1.849998683	8
3. Alim	8	0.333333333	0.22296544	0.787401575	0.505183508	46
4. Alangas	22	1	0.613154961	2.362204724	1.487679843	13
5. Antipolo	13	1	0.362318841	2.362204724	1.362261782	19
6. Anulailalaki	1	0.333333333	0.02787068	0.787401575	0.407636127	60
7. Anchoandilaw	35	0.666666667	0.975473802	1.57480315	1.275138476	22
8. Avocado	5	0.666666667	0.1393534	1.57480315	0.857078275	33
9. Bayabas	22	1	0.613154961	2.362204724	1.487679843	13
10. Bagras	14	0.333333333	0.390189521	0.787401575	0.588795548	38
11. Banato	3	0.333333333	0.08361204	0.787401575	0.435506807	50
12. Bangkal	32	0.666666667	0.891861761	1.57480315	1.233332456	24

No.	Name						
13.	Botong	1	0.333333333	0.02787068	0.787401575	0.407636127	60
14.	Binunga	10	0.333333333	0.2787068	0.787401575	0.533054188	42
15.	Caimito	10	0.666666667	0.2787068	1.57480315	0.926754975	29
16.	Cacao	1	0.333333333	0.02787068	0.787401575	0.407636127	60
17.	Dao	8	0.666666667	0.22296544	1.57480315	0.898884295	31
18.	Durian	6	0.333333333	0.16722408	0.787401575	0.477312828	48
19.	Fire tree	7	0.666666667	0.19509476	1.57480315	0.884948955	32
20.	Golden Shower	12	0.333333333	0.334448161	0.787401575	0.560924868	40
21.	Guayabano	42	1	1.170568562	2.362204724	1.766386643	9
22.	Yemane	363	1	10.11705686	2.362204724	6.23963079	3
23.	Hanagdong	30	1	0.836120401	2.362204724	1.599162563	11
24.	Hagimit	1	0.333333333	0.02787068	0.787401575	0.407636127	60
25.	Hauili	2	0.666666667	0.05574136	1.57480315	0.815272255	36
26.	Ipil-ipil	70	1	1.950947603	2.362204724	2.156576164	7
27.	Ipil	9	0.333333333	0.25083612	0.787401575	0.519118848	45
28.	Igyo	8	0.333333333	0.22296544	0.787401575	0.505183508	46
29.	Indian tree	62	0.666666667	1.727982163	1.57480315	1.651392656	10
30.	Indian rubber tree	3	0.333333333	0.08361204	0.787401575	0.435506807	50
31.	Ilang – ilang	2	0.333333333	0.05574136	0.787401575	0.421571467	55
32.	Jackfruit	274	1	7.636566332	2.362204724	4.999385528	4
33.	Kamagong	13	0.333333333	0.362318841	0.787401575	0.574860208	39
34.	Kamatchili	10	0.333333333	0.2787068	0.787401575	0.533054188	42
35.	Kamansi	13	1	0.362318841	2.362204724	1.362261782	19
36.	Calamansan ai	4	0.666666667	0.11148272	1.57480315	0.843142935	35
37.	Kalukoi	3	0.333333333	0.08361204	0.787401575	0.435506807	50
38.	Kapok	14	0.666666667	0.390189521	1.57480315	0.982496335	27
39.	Kupang	2	0.333333333	0.05574136	0.787401575	0.421571467	55
40.	Lanzones	3	0.333333333	0.08361204	0.787401575	0.435506807	50
41.	Lukban/pomelo	24	1	0.668896321	2.362204724	1.515550523	12
42.	Lumbang	4	0.333333333	0.11148272	0.787401575	0.449442147	49

No.	Species						
43.	Mahogany	948	1	26.421404 68	2.36220472 4	14.39180 47	1
44.	Mangosteen	2	0.33333 3333	0.0557413 6	0.78740157 5	0.421571 467	55
45.	Malabagang	1	0.33333 3333	0.0278706 8	0.78740157 5	0.407636 127	60
46.	Mangga Group	838	1	23.355629 88	2.36220472 4	12.85891 73	2
47.	Malapapaya	17	0.66666 6667	0.4738015 61	1.57480315	1.024302 355	26
48.	Matangara w	1	0.33333 3333	0.0278706 8	0.78740157 5	0.407636 127	60
49.	Molave	2	0.33333 3333	0.0557413 6	0.78740157 5	0.421571 467	55
50.	Narra	136	1	3.7904124 86	2.36220472 4	3.076308 605	6
51.	Neem tree	18	0.66666 6667	0.5016722 41	1.57480315	1.038237 695	25
52.	Niog – niogan	2	0.33333 3333	0.0557413 6	0.78740157 5	0.421571 467	55
53.	Norfolk pine	5	0.66666 6667	0.1393534	1.57480315	0.857078 275	33
54.	Para rubber	34	0.66666 6667	0.9476031 22	1.57480315	1.261203 136	23
55.	Palosanto	1	0.33333 3333	0.0278706 8	0.78740157 5	0.407636 127	60
56.	Philippine Chesnut	3	0.33333 3333	0.0836120 4	0.78740157 5	0.435506 807	50
57.	Rain tree	183	1	5.1003344 48	2.36220472 4	3.731269 586	5
58.	Rambutan	10	0.66666 6667	0.2787068	1.57480315	0.926754 975	29
59.	Red river gum	23	0.33333 3333	0.6410256 41	0.78740157 5	0.714213 608	37
60.	Santol	15	1	0.4180602 01	2.36220472 4	1.390132 463	18
61.	Sablut	1	0.33333 3333	0.0278706 8	0.78740157 5	0.407636 127	60
62.	Sampalok	19	1	0.5295429 21	2.36220472 4	1.445873 823	16
63.	Saraca	1	0.33333 3333	0.0278706 8	0.78740157 5	0.407636 127	60
64.	Sibukaw	1	0.33333 3333	0.0278706 8	0.78740157 5	0.407636 127	60
65.	Sinigwilas	11	0.33333 3333	0.3065774 8	0.78740157 5	0.546989 528	41
66.	Tambis	1	0.33333 3333	0.0278706 8	0.78740157 5	0.407636 127	60
67.	Tangisangb ayawak	21	1	0.5852842 81	2.36220472 4	1.473744 503	15
68.	Talisai	11	0.66666 6667	0.3065774 8	1.57480315	0.940690 315	28
69.	Tan – ag	47	0.66666 6667	1.3099219 62	1.57480315	1.442362 556	17

70.	Teak	10	1	0.2787068	2.362204724	1.320455762	21
71.	White lauan	10	0.333333333	0.2787068	0.787401575	0.533054188	42
72.	YakalSaplongan	1	0.333333333	0.02787068	0.787401575	0.407636127	60
OVER ALL TOTAL		3588	42.33333333	100	100	100	

Table 3 Showed that there were three thousand five hundred eighty eight (3,588) individuals or stands found inside the study site. Mahogany has a total number of individuals of 948 with Importance Value of 14.39, Mangga group with 838 stands with Importance Value of 12.85, Yemane has 363 stands with 6.2 Importance Value and Jackfruit with 274 stands with 4.99 Importance Value.

Table 4. Shannon Diversity Index

SPECIES	TOTAL POPULATION	DIVERSITY INDEX	Relative Dominant species %	RANK
Mangium	1	-0.002281313	0.02787068	
African Tulip	48	-0.057714371	1.337792642	
Alim	8	-0.013614066	0.22296544	
Alangas	22	-0.031236001	0.613154961	
Antipolo	13	-0.020363771	0.362318841	
Anulailalaki	1	-0.002281313	0.02787068	
Anchoandilaw	35	-0.045164458	0.975473802	
Avocado	5	-0.009163757	0.1393534	
Bayabas	22	-0.031236001	0.613154961	
Bagras	14	-	0.3901	

		0.021641054	89521	
Banato	3	-0.005925366	0.08361204	
Bangkal	32	-0.042092435	0.89861761	
Botong	1	-0.002281313	0.02787068	
Binunga	10	-0.016395666	0.2787068	
Caimito	10	-0.016395666	0.2787068	
Cacao	1	-0.002281313	0.02787068	
Dao	8	-0.013614066	0.22296544	
Durian	6	-0.010691623	0.16722408	
Fire tree	7	-0.012172821	0.19509476	
Golden Shower	12	-0.019065029	0.33448161	
Guayabano	42	-0.052063151	1.170568562	

Yemane	363	-0.23177645	10.117 05686	3
Hanagdong	30	-0.040001278	0.8361 20401	
Hagimit	1	-0.002281313	0.0278 7068	
Hauili	2	-0.004176256	0.0557 4136	
Ipil-ipil	70	-0.076805978	1.9509 47603	
Ipil	9	-0.015020382	0.2508 3612	
Igyo	8	-0.013614066	0.2229 6544	
Indian tree	62	-0.070125246	1.7279 82163	
Indian rubber tree	3	-0.005925366	0.0836 1204	
Ilang – ilang	2	-0.004176256	0.0557 4136	
Jackfruit	274	-0.196429448	7.6365 66332	4
Kamagong	13	-0.020363771	0.3623 18841	

Kamatchili	10	-0.016395666	0.2787068	
Kamansi	13	-0.020363771	0.362318841	
Calamansanai	4	-0.007579772	0.11148272	
Kalukoi	3	-0.005925366	0.08361204	
Kapok	14	-0.021641054	0.390189521	
Kupang	2	-0.004176256	0.05574136	
Lansones	3	-0.005925366	0.08361204	
Lukban/pomelo	24	-0.033493621	0.668896321	
Lumbang	4	-0.007579772	0.11148272	
Mahogany	948	-0.351667766	26.42140468	1
Mangosteen	2	-0.004176256	0.05574136	
Malabagang	1	-0.002281313	0.02787068	

Mangga Group	838	-0.339668428	23.35562988	2
Malapapaya	17	-0.025358508	0.473801561	
Matangaraw	1	-0.002281313	0.02787068	
Molave	2	-0.004176256	0.05574136	
Narra	136	-0.124048653	3.790412486	6
Neem tree	18	-0.026563437	0.501672241	
Niog – niogan	2	-0.004176256	0.05574136	
Norfolk pine	5	-0.009163757	0.1393534	
Para rubber	34	-0.044148732	0.947603122	
Palosanto	1	-0.002281313	0.02787068	
Philippine Chesnut	3	-0.005925366	0.08361204	
Rain tree	183	-0.15177902	5.100334448	5

Rambutan	10	-0.016395666	0.2787068	
Red river gum	23	-0.032370872	0.641025641	
Santol	15	-0.022898411	0.418060201	
Sablut	1	-0.002281313	0.02787068	
Sampalok	19	-0.027752874	0.529542921	
Saraca	1	-0.002281313	0.02787068	
Sibukaw	1	-0.002281313	0.02787068	
Sinigwilas	11	-0.017743034	0.30657748	
Tambis	1	-0.002281313	0.02787068	
Tangisang bayawak	21	-0.030088457	0.585284281	
Talisai	11	-0.017743034	0.30657748	
Tan – ag	47	-0.056787771	1.309921962	

Teak	**10**	-0.016395666	0.2787068	
White lauan	**10**	-0.016395666	0.2787068	
YakalSapl ongan	**1**	-0.002281313	0.02787068	
OVER ALL TOTAL	3,588	2.595125399	100	

Table 4 showed that that there were three thousand five hundred eighty eight (3,588) individuals or stands found inside the study site. Mahogany has a diversity index of 26.4, Mangga group with diversity index of 23.35, Yemane has Diversity Index of 10.11 and Jackfruit with 7.6 Diversity Index, a total of 2.59 Shannon Diversity which means that the area is moderately diverse.

SUMMARY, CONCLUSION AND RECOMMENDATIONS

SUMMARY

The general objectives of the study was to find out the statuses and existence of tree flora species their classification and species diversity. It was conducted at the Mindanao State University - Maguindanao Campus, Datu Odin Sinsuat, Maguindanao, using a Transect walk method with an area of forty two (42) hectares with 3 stations.

FINDINGS

A study entitled "Tree Flora of Mindanao State University – Maguindanao Campus" was conducted on October 20 to November 5, 2019 at the MSU – Maguindanao Campus, Datu Odin Sinsuat, Maguindanao, using Transect walk method, and findings are as follows:

- In terms of number of tree species there are three thousand five hundred eighty eight (3,588) individuals or stands.

- There were seventy five (75) tree species under twenty five (25) families.

- Fabaceae has 11 species, Moraceae has 10 species, Euphorbiaceae has 7 species and Anacardiaceae has 6 species.

- Conservation status with thirty (30) vulnerable, fourteen (14) least concern, twelve (12) critically endangered, nine (9) endangered, (3) three data deficient, three (3) other wildlife species, two (2) not evaluated, (1) one threatened and one (1) near threatened.

- Ecological status of forty seven (47) endemic, twenty six (26) exotic, and two (2) invasive.

- The most dominant species is Mahogany (*Swieteniamahogani*) with 948 stands, Importance value of 14.39 and Shannon Diversity Index of 26.42, followed by Mango (*Mangiferaindica*) with 838 stands, Importance Value of 12.85 and a value of 23.35 Shannon Diversity Index.

- Lanipau (*Terminaliafoetidissima*) has the highest average diameter of 102.76 cm while Rain tree (*Samaneasaman*) has the highest average height of 46.3 meters.

- Shannon Diversity Index has a total value of 2.59 which means the study area has moderately diverse.

- These trees surround the area of Mindanao State University – Maguindanao Campus should be conserved and protected for the sustainability of the vegetation and habitat for other life forms.

CONCLUSION:

There are seventy two (72) species of trees under 25 families. Most of them belong to endemic and some were exotic species and threatened.

Based from the observation, the dominant trees are Mahogany, Mango, and Yemane. The area was moderately diverse. The species with high importance value are Mahogany, Mango and Yemane.

RECOMMENDATION:

- Massive tree planting of tree species that dominate the area like Mahogany, Mango and Yemane.

- The administration must make an ordinance to prohibit timber poachers/poaching, firewood gathers and charcoal makers in the vicinity area of MSU-MAGUINDANAO

- The administration must implement the existing local and national policies on the preservation and protection of the remaining tree species in MSU-MAGUINDANAO.

- As an advocacy people should be aware to the importance of forest resources especially on trees.

- Further study should be conducted on another side or aspect of the MSU-MAGUINDANAO.

LITERATURE CITED

Torres, 2011. Tree Identification Manual.

Aribal, N.D. Guide to Tree Identification volume 1 ISBN - 978-971-0435-0

E.S Fernando, B.Y Sun, M.H Shu, H.Y Kong, K.S Koh, N.D. Flowering Plants and Ferns of Mount Makiling, ASEAN-Korean Environmental Cooperation Unit

La Frankie, 2010. Trees of Tropical Asia Vol. 1 & 2, 2010

Retrieved from:https://www.iucnredlist.org/
Retrieved from:http://www.stuartxchange.org/index.html
Retrieved   from: https://pdfs.semanticscholar.org/af12/e88e02d42774853ddc c89f5cd3b2c5a417a4.pdf
Retrieved from:http://www.treesaregood.com/treecare/resources/benef itstrees.pdf;2011(1998,2004)
Retrieved   from: International   Society   of Arboriculture.http://www.pnh.com.ph/category/4- Articles/34-flora-of-the-Philippines-page-1.html;Digital
Retrieved from:https://www.philippineplants.org/PhilippinePlants.htm l

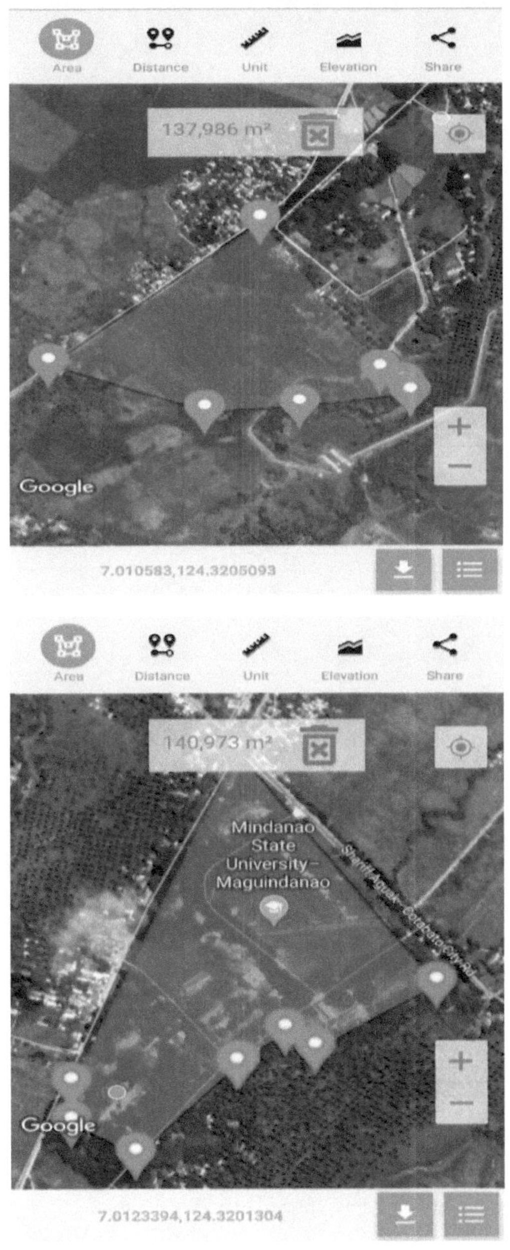

These maps were the study area

LIMBARO/LAURIE 2020